HIGHER LOVE

Discovering God's Design for Your Marriage

PARTICIPANT'S GUIDE

D1226141

FOCUS THE FAMILY

TYNDALE HOUSE PUBLISHERS, INC.
Carol Stream, Illinois

CONTENTS

QUICK START GUIDE FOR COUPLES

Whether you're studying in a group, as a couple, or individually, this book is for you. It's packed with discussion questions, advice, biblical input, and application activities.

But maybe all you'd like to do right now is watch the accompanying DVD and talk about it with your spouse. If so, go directly to the "Catching the Vision" section of each chapter. There you'll find the discussion questions you're looking for.

When you have more time, we encourage you to explore the other features in this book. We think you'll find them . . . essential!

For even more help with your relationship, go to
focusonthefamily.com/marriage.

WELCOME!

If there's anything you don't need, it's one more thing to do.

Unless, of course, that one thing might make the *other* things a whole lot easier.

We can't guarantee that this course will take all the challenge out of your marriage. It won't keep you from forgetting your anniversary, thaw all the icy silences, or make your spouse alphabetize the shoes in your closet.

But it *will* help you understand why you're married, how to stay that way, and how to enjoy it to the fullest. That's because you'll learn the essentials—what's vital to a healthy relationship, keys to working out your differences, and what God considers most important in "holy matrimony."

In other words, you'll discover how to be the husband or wife you really want to be.

That takes effort, but it doesn't take boredom or busy work. So we've designed this course to be provocative and practical. At its heart is an entertaining, down-to-earth video series featuring many of today's most popular marriage experts. And in your hands is the book that's going to make it all personal for you—the Participant's Guide.

In each chapter of this book, you'll find the following sections:

Finding Yourself. Take this survey to figure out where you stand on the subject at hand.

Catching the Vision. Use this section as you watch and think about the DVD.

Digging Deeper. This Bible study includes Scripture passages and thought-provoking questions.

Making It Work. Practice makes perfect, so here's your chance to begin applying principles from the DVD to your own marriage.

Bringing It Home. To wrap up, a licensed counselor affiliated with Focus on the Family offers encouraging advice you can use this week.

Whether you're using this book as part of a group or on your own, taking a few minutes to read and complete each chapter will bring the messages of the DVD home.

And isn't that exactly where you and your spouse need it most?

Note: Many issues addressed in this series are difficult ones. Some couples may need to address them in greater detail and depth. The DVD presentations and this guide are intended as general advice only, and not to replace clinical counseling, medical treatment, legal counsel, or financial guidance.

Focus on the Family maintains a referral network of Christian counselors. For information, call 1-800-A-FAMILY and ask for the counseling department. You can also download free, printable brochures offering help for couples at http://www.focusonthefamily.com/marriage/articles/brochures.aspx.

Chapter 1

FINDING HOLINESS AND HAPPINESS

When Kay and Carl married, they made a commitment to honor each other. They hoped nothing could break their bond. They had high moral values and a personal relationship with the Lord. Their security was in Jesus—not in themselves, not in each other.

They were beginning in the right direction. Could they stay the course?

It didn't take Kay long to realize that Carl had a lot of faults she'd failed to recognize. One was his inept handling of their money.

Kay had a choice. She could handle the problem in a way that was consistent with her faith, which took the authority of the Bible seriously. Or she could turn elsewhere for advice.

Every marriage needs a bond to sustain it during the trials that will surface. Is faith in Christ really the glue that can keep a marriage together? How does a biblical worldview make a difference?

—Betty Jordan
Licensed Professional Counselor[1]

Identifying Your Needs

Take a few minutes to fill out the following survey.

1. How might each of the following describe your wedding in 10 words
   or less? Why?
   your maid of honor _____
   your best man _____
   your parents _____
   your pastor _____
   God _____

2. How would you rank the following elements of marriage from
   most important to least? How do you think God would rank these
   factors? If the rankings are different, what do you think accounts for
   that?
   ___ whether spouses agree on political issues
   ___ how often spouses pray together
   ___ whether spouses plan to have children
   ___ how involved spouses are in ministry
   ___ how much spouses enjoy each other's company
   ___ how much money spouses give to church work

3. How do you think each of the following would define marriage?
   your spouse _____
   Jesus Christ _____
   someone who's been married a dozen times _____
   your kids, if you have any _____
   your oldest living relative _____

4. Did your wedding ceremony acknowledge God's involvement in your marriage? If so, how? If not, why not? _____

_____

5. Since your wedding, have you acknowledged God's involvement in your marriage? If so, how? If not, why not? _____

_____

Watching and Discussing the DVD

Why did God invent marriage? To make us happy? Not according to author Gary Thomas, whose ideas about wedded bliss in this video segment may turn your assumptions upside-down.

God is more interested in making us *holy*, Gary explains, and marriage is a great place to work on that. As if that's not enough, Gary urges husbands and wives to see God not only as their Father—but also their Father-in-law. That's because our spouses are God's children, and we're to treat them that way.

Dr. Greg Smalley adds a story from his own marriage, rounding out a thought-provoking look at why you got married—even if you didn't know it at the time.

After viewing the DVD, use questions like these to help you think through what you saw and heard.

1. If you stood on a street corner in your town and asked people, "Why did God invent marriage?" what would they answer? If you surveyed 100 of those people, how many do you think would give you replies like each of the following? Why?

- "For raising children."
- "So we wouldn't be lonely."
- "To torture us."
- "To make us better people."
- "Who said He invented marriage?"

2. Gary Thomas believes God created marriage to make us holy, not just to make us happy. Which of the following best describes your reaction to that idea?
   - "That figures, since God doesn't want anyone to be happy."
   - "It doesn't seem to be working."
   - "Being happy is a result of being holy."
   - "That explains why I'm so miserable."
   - other _____

3. How was Gary's experience with the ice trays an example of a spiritual challenge in marriage? What do you think God wanted him to do in that situation? Why?

4. Who's one of the holiest people you've ever met? Was he or she also one of the happiest? Does that make you interested in holiness? Why or why not?

5. What do you think you could learn about loving, giving, forgiving, confronting, or asking forgiveness in each of the following situations?
   - Your spouse blames you when the restaurant you chose for dinner has a long waiting list.
   - You borrow your spouse's cell phone and discover that he or she's been getting calls from an old flame.
   - Your spouse can't seem to give up smoking, and you have asthma.

6. Gary says that many people expect their spouses to give them fulfill-
   ment, joy, and unconditional love—which only God can provide reli-
   ably. If you gave up those expectations tomorrow morning, how might
   the rest of your week be different?

7. If you really believe your spouse is God's child, and that He's protec-
   tive of him or her, how will it affect what you do in the following
   situations?
   - You wish your spouse would lose 20 pounds.
   - Your spouse forgets to pay the car insurance bill,
     then gets in a fender bender after coverage lapses.
   - Your spouse is accused of shoplifting.

8. According to Gary, we need to accept the following three spiritual
   realities about marriage. Which of them is hardest for you to understand? To accept? To remember during everyday disappointments and
   conflicts?
   - Marriage is a very difficult relationship.
   - You stay married even though your spouse isn't
     perfect.
   - God is your spiritual Father-in-law, and you love
     your spouse out of reverence for Him.

9. Why does Gary sometimes pray when he wakes up about loving his
   wife more than anyone else does? How would you put that message
   in the form of a prayer about your spouse? How often would you be
   willing to pray it?

Bible Study

> The LORD God said, "It is not good for the man to be alone. I will make a helper suitable for him." . . .
>
> So the man gave names to all the livestock, the birds of the air and all the beasts of the field.
>
> But for Adam no suitable helper was found. So the LORD God caused the man to fall into a deep sleep; and while he was sleeping, he took one of the man's ribs and closed up the place with flesh. Then the LORD God made a woman from the rib he had taken out of the man, and he brought her to the man.
>
> The man said,
> "This is now bone of my bones
> and flesh of my flesh;
> she shall be called 'woman,'
> for she was taken out of man."
>
> For this reason a man will leave his father and mother and be united to his wife, and they will become one flesh.
>
> The man and his wife were both naked, and they felt no shame.
> (Genesis 2:18, 20-25)

1. Do you think God expected to find a "suitable helper" for Adam in the animal kingdom? Why or why not?

2. Why do you suppose God took Eve out of Adam, only to decree that they reunite again? What does this tell you about God's purposes for marriage?

3. Is it hard to imagine feeling "no shame" about being naked? Why or why not? Do you think that's still true of most husbands and wives? Why or why not?

4. If Genesis 2:18, 20-25 were the only thing you knew about men and women, how would you describe God's view of marriage?

> *When Jesus had finished saying these things, he left Galilee and went into the region of Judea to the other side of the Jordan. Large crowds followed him, and he healed them there.*
>
> *Some Pharisees came to him to test him. They asked, "Is it lawful for a man to divorce his wife for any and every reason?"*
>
> *"Haven't you read," he replied, "that at the beginning the Creator 'made them male and female,' and said, 'For this reason a man will leave his father and mother and be united to his wife, and the two will become one flesh'? So they are no longer two, but one. Therefore what God has joined together, let man not separate."*
>
> *"Why then," they asked, "did Moses command that a man give his wife a certificate of divorce and send her away?"*
>
> *Jesus replied, "Moses permitted you to divorce your wives because your hearts were hard. But it was not this way from the beginning. I tell you that anyone who divorces his wife, except for marital unfaithfulness, and marries another woman commits adultery."*
>
> *The disciples said to him, "If this is the situation between a husband and wife, it is better not to marry."*
>
> *Jesus replied, "Not everyone can accept this word, but only those to whom it has been given. For some are eunuchs because they were born that way; others were made that way by men; and others have renounced marriage because of the kingdom of heaven. The one who can accept this should accept it." (Matthew 19:1-12)*

5. Is it lawful today to divorce "for any and every reason"? What reasons do most divorcing couples give?

6. Why did the disciples think Jesus' view of marriage made singleness look good? Do you think most people would agree? Why or why not?

7. If Matthew 19:1-12 were the only thing you knew about men and women, how would you describe God's view of marriage?

8. If you believe that God Himself has joined you and your spouse together, how might this affect your reactions to the following situations?
    - You disagree strongly over whether to buy a house.
    - You're tired of spending holidays with your in-laws.
    - Your spouse is diagnosed with Alzheimer's.
    - The two of you are asked to start a small group for your church.
    - Your spouse warns that the two of you are "drifting apart."

Applying the Principles

This chapter's DVD segment urges couples to seek holiness, which leads to real happiness. Does that sound good to you—or like something you'd rather avoid?

It depends on your attitude toward holiness and happiness. To help you and your spouse discuss these two concepts, try coming up with a "Happiness Meal" and a "Holiness Meal."

Most of us know what a "Happy Meal" is. But what would you put in a "Happiness Meal" and a "Holiness Meal"?

Would you put junk food in the Happiness Meal? Comfort food, perhaps? Would you put health food in the Holiness Meal? Or leave the bag empty and give the money to hunger relief?

Is there a meal that would qualify as both?

Here are menu items to choose from. You can choose up to six items per meal; write them on the blanks next to the appropriate bag.

Chicken nuggets

Milkshake

Broccoli

Tofu

Salad

Raw onions

Candy bar

Double cheeseburger

Diet soda

French fries

Other _____

Deep-fried macaroni and cheese bites

Granola

Nothing

Oyster crackers and grape juice

Onion rings

Filet mignon

Peanut butter and jelly sandwich

Water

Regular soda

Prunes

_____   _____

_____   _____

_____   _____

_____   _____

_____   _____

When you're done, compare your choices to those of your spouse if possible. Then discuss the following:

Based on our meal choices, what do we think makes us happy? How has that been reflected in the way we spend time as a couple?

When we think of holiness, do we think of depriving or punishing ourselves?

What attitudes about these two concepts might we need to examine or overcome before we can practice what we've learned in this session?

Encouragement from a Counselor

Remember Kay, who had to choose whether to handle her marital problem with God's view in mind?

She decided to take an approach that echoed 1 Peter 3:3-6: "Your beauty . . . should be that of your inner self, the unfading beauty of a gentle and quiet spirit, which is of great worth in God's sight. For this is the way the holy women of the past who put their hope in God used to make themselves beautiful. They were submissive to their own husbands, like Sarah, who obeyed Abraham and called him her master. You are her daughters if you do what is right and do not give way to fear."

When Kay respectfully and graciously confronted Carl with their dilemma, he was able to hear her instead of being defensive. Now it was his turn to decide whether his response would reflect his faith.

He decided to apply principles he'd learned in 1 Timothy 3:3-6, especially the instructions to be gentle, not quarrelsome or proud or greedy. In particular, he didn't allow pride to get in the way of learning new budgeting methods.

In other words, faith helped keep them together.

Then came another challenge. Carl and Kay moved to another state, leaving the church that had been an awesome support system for them. Knowing what a difference faith had made to them individually and as a couple, they looked in their new location for the nurturing and fellowship of other believers. They found it in a church with solid teaching, where they began to volunteer. Again their faith provided resources that strengthened their relationship.

Faith helps keep couples together despite the smaller challenges of everyday life, too. When Carl offends Kay, for example, her understanding of what the Bible says about forgiveness is activated. So is her commitment to apply those principles. She knows that God has graciously extended forgiveness to her, and expects her to do the same for others (Matthew 18:23-35). This helps her to have a forgiving heart toward Carl, preventing a root of bitterness—a marriage killer—from taking hold. Forgiveness is a vital ingredient of the glue that holds marriages together.

So is fidelity. Carl and Kay have pledged to be faithful to one another, which might prove difficult for Carl in his job. He works with women who are congenial and attractive. All the temptations are there—travel, creative teamwork, the opportunity to share confidences. Carl isn't blind, but the eyes of his heart are enlightened (Ephesians 1:18). Having received the gift of a relationship with God, he's not about to mess it up. He chooses to "Avoid every kind of evil" (1 Thessalonians 5:22). His commitment to Kay flows from his commitment to the Lord.

If you're a follower of Christ, staying together as a couple involves the same things that living your faith does—constantly putting aside pride, working daily on fully accepting God's forgiveness, and seeking to do what pleases Him. The following passage applies to marriage as it does to all of life: "Therefore, since we are surrounded by such a great cloud of witnesses, let us throw off everything that hinders and the sin that so easily entangles, and let us run with perseverance the race marked out for us" (Hebrews 12:1).

Can faith keep you together? God's Word says it can.

—Betty Jordan
Licensed Professional Counselor[2]

Chapter 2

IT'S NOT ABOUT YOU

When Tyler married Kat, he thought he knew what a Christian home looked like.

He didn't want one.

When he was growing up, his family went to church regularly and adopted many cultural symptoms of Christianity. They had plaques with Scripture verses, cars with fish symbols, and attended religious conferences.

Behind closed doors, however, family members rarely spoke of Christ. They prayed only at mealtimes, and lost track of their Bibles between Sundays. Unlike their winsome public image, they were often in conflict.

If that was a Christian home, Tyler wasn't interested in recreating it.

If you're a Christian, you probably agree that the source of joy is Christ. You probably believe that when you're busy enjoying Him, your home will be happy. But that's pretty lofty. We need some handles to really pick up this idea.

—Rob Jackson
Licensed Professional Counselor[3]

Identifying Your Needs

Here are some questions to help you discover where you stand on this session's topic.

1. When you hear someone talk about "God's view of marriage," which of the following best describes your reaction? Why?

    ___ "Who cares?"

    ___ "How interesting that 'God's view' just happens to be yours."

    ___ "I wish I could know what He thinks of my marriage."

    ___ "With all due respect, He's not down here in the trenches."

    ___ "He wants to turn my marriage into a Sunday school class."

    ___ "I want to know His view and let it change the way we live."

    ___ other _____

2. Which of the following sources are you most likely to turn to for marriage advice? Why?

    ___ friends

    ___ a TV or radio host

    ___ Christian counselor

    ___ non-Christian counselor

    ___ pastor

    ___ the Bible

    ___ another book

    ___ other _____

3. How might your marriage be different if you lived in the following times and places? Do you think it would better reflect God's view of marriage? Why or why not?

    ___ the Garden of Eden

___ Victorian England

___ ancient Israel

___ the U.S. during World War II

___ present-day Afghanistan

___ an international space station in the year 2050

4. Do you believe spouses with a biblical view of marriage are happier than other spouses? Why or why not? _____

_____

5. Do you think it matters whether they're happier, as long as they're "right"? Why or why not? _____

_____

6. When you got married, did you have a biblical view of marriage? If so, how did you get it? If not, what difference might it have made if you did? _____

Watching and Discussing the DVD

What does the inventor of marriage have to say about it? Why did He bring Adam and Eve together?

Dr. Del Tackett, president of the Focus on the Family Institute and presenter of *The Truth Project*, explains in this DVD segment how God's view of marriage counts the most—and not just because it "works best." Marriage, he says, is a picture of the relationship among the members of the Trinity.

We can't change that—and wouldn't want to, once we begin to grasp its importance.

After viewing the DVD, use questions like these to help you think through what you saw and heard.

1. How would you compare the biblical view of marriage to the perspective offered by the following TV shows? Do you think God's view would make a good premise for a sitcom? Why or why not?
   - *Trading Spouses*
   - *'Til Death*
   - *The Simpsons*
   - *Desperate Housewives*

2. Dr. Del Tackett calls marriage a sacrificial relationship. If it were legally defined this way, do you think fewer people would get married? Why or why not?

3. A self-centered view of marriage leads us to try to get our own way. Which spouse do you think would get his or her own way in each of the following situations? Why? How might the struggle affect each marriage?
   - A wife who wants to have children tries to "guilt" her husband (who doesn't want to have children) into changing his mind.
   - A husband who wants to host a home Bible study tells his wife (who doesn't want to host one) that the decision is his because he's the spiritual leader of the family.
   - A wife who wants to spend $5,000 redecorating the living room tries to pressure her husband (who wants to spend $500) by withholding sex.
   - A husband who wants sex more frequently tries to pressure his wife (who wants less) by refusing to talk to her unless absolutely necessary.

4. According to Del, one of the purposes of marriage is to glorify God. How could a husband and wife glorify God in the way they handle the following problems?
    - not being able to have biological children
    - living next door to a woman whose dog barks all the time
    - taking care of a parent who has Parkinson's disease
    - being criticized for having an interracial marriage

5. Del says our marriages are meant to reflect the Trinity's awesome unity, intimacy, relationship, and fellowship. Which of those qualities have you seen in another couple's marriage, if only in a small way? What effect has that had on you?

6. Del warns against an "I want what I want" attitude. Which of the following have you heard at home? Do they always reflect a "my way" mindset? Why or why not?
    - "It's my turn."
    - "Don't tell me what to do."
    - "You're not my mother."
    - "I don't have to put up with this."
    - other _____

Bible Study

> *Submit to one another out of reverence for Christ.*
>
> *Wives, submit to your husbands as to the Lord. For the husband is the head of the wife as Christ is the head of the church, his body, of which he is the Savior. Now as the church submits to Christ, so also wives should submit to their husbands in everything.*

Husbands, love your wives, just as Christ loved the church and gave himself up for her to make her holy, cleansing her by the washing with water through the word, and to present her to himself as a radiant church, without stain or wrinkle or any other blemish, but holy and blameless. In this same way, husbands ought to love their wives as their own bodies. He who loves his wife loves himself. After all, no one ever hated his own body, but he feeds and cares for it, just as Christ does the church—for we are members of his body. "For this reason a man will leave his father and mother and be united to his wife, and the two will become one flesh." This is a profound mystery—but I am talking about Christ and the church. However, each one of you also must love his wife as he loves himself, and the wife must respect her husband. (Ephesians 5:21-33)

1. How is marriage "a profound mystery" to you? How is it not? Do the mysterious parts tend to cause the most trouble, or the more easily explained parts? Can you give an example?

2. Are there any words in this passage that bother you? If so, can you explain your reaction?

3. What are the differences between the terms in each of the following pairs? Why are the differences important in a marriage?
   - *submit* and *grovel*
   - *love* and *fondness*
   - *respect* and *fear*
   - *holy* and *perfect*
   - *head* and *boss*

4. How would you describe the relationship between Christ and the church? How is it like the relationship between spouses? How is it different?

Applying the Principles

Let's say the following events happen to you tomorrow. How would you react? In the blanks, describe your perspective on each event—and what you think God's view might be.

6:00 A.M.: Alarm doesn't go off. Your spouse inadvertently unplugged it last night, thinking he or she was holding the cord to the cell phone charger.

Your perspective _____

God's perspective _____

7:00 A.M.: Running late for work. No time for breakfast, only for a piece of cold pizza.

Your perspective _____

God's perspective _____

7:59 A.M.: You get a $50 ticket for going 43 miles per hour in a 35-miles-per-hour zone.

Your perspective _____

God's perspective _____

9:17 A.M.: In staff meeting, boss names you employee of the month. You'll get to park closer to the building for 30 days, and receive a $50 gift card to your favorite coffee shop.

Your perspective _____

God's perspective _____

11:32 A.M.: Spouse calls, says that if you've gotten over your hissy fit about the alarm not going off, you can meet for lunch. You reply that you've got too much work to do, which isn't quite true.

Your perspective _____
God's perspective _____

12:09 P.M.: Spouse sees you in a restaurant at lunch with two co-workers. Gives you "the look" and leaves, obviously unhappy.

Your perspective _____
God's perspective _____

2:46 P.M.: In a meeting, you make a joke about marriage—comparing it to a minimum-security prison.

Your perspective _____
God's perspective _____

4:38 P.M.: You leave work early, intending to pick up a small "peace-making" gift for your spouse. But when you hear a talk radio show about thoughtless spouses, you get mad again and change your mind.

Your perspective _____
God's perspective _____

5:59 P.M.: Spouse has left a message about being late for dinner. You have another piece of cold pizza.

Your perspective _____
God's perspective _____

7:00 P.M.: Spouse gets home, but neither of you seems to want to talk. You watch TV alone.

Your perspective _____
God's perspective _____

10:51 P.M.: Still watching TV. Spouse has fallen asleep. You vow to have a conversation about this . . . sometime.

Your perspective _____
God's perspective _____

With your mate if possible, compare your perspective on the events to God's view. How are they different? How do our priorities tend to differ from God's?

Discuss with your spouse what both of you can do to keep God's perspective in mind this week. Is there something you can carry in your wallet, purse, or pocket to remind you of His view? How might this affect the way you relate to each other?

You may also want to read John 17 at home this week. What might happen to a husband and wife who read that chapter once a week and asked whether their marriage reflected that kind of oneness? What are two or three other Bible passages that you and your spouse could read to measure how your relationship is doing from God's perspective? How often would you want to read them?

Encouragement from a Counselor

Many couples would like to create a "Christian home." Or they've been told that it's important to do so. But what is a Christian home really like? Here are some ideas.

1. *A Christian home is gracious.* Home should be a safe place to mess up. Family members need the ointment of grace on the wounds of their hearts, remembering perfection is not the goal. With the world firing at you, make your home a foxhole for retreat and healing.

Grace invites humility and repentance. Scripture tells us God's kindness leads us to repentance (Romans 2:4). When a spouse or other family member wrongs you, approach that person gently. Offering grace will come back to you many times as you mess up in the future.

Gracious language says, "I expect the best of you." It avoids criticism, sarcasm, and snide humor at all times. Instead of praising only performance, it encourages, notices, and rewards effort.

2. *A Christian home is a place of service.* If you're a parent, you've tasted sacrificial service. Anyone who cleans a helpless, soiled infant or forgoes sleep to feed a hungry baby knows servanthood on a very practical level.

But why wait until parenthood? What would happen if you served your spouse from betrothal forward? Acts of kindness, respect, and self-control should flavor the Christian home. This is where husbands and wives find that serving each other in Christ is primary. Serving others is important, too—but integrity at home is foundational.

Christ-centered couples can discover that all of life is sacred. The mundane duties of laundry, bill paying, housekeeping, and lawn mowing become opportunities to serve God. This can transform your marriage, teach your children by example, and bypass many conflicts.

3. *A Christian home practices spiritual disciplines.* Happy families are growing spiritually. Fellowship with Christ through the Scriptures plays a central role in a home's peace. A Christian home is where you learn how to live as you study, meditate, and pray your way through the Bible.

Spiritual growth includes discovering the high value of worship. No longer relegated to certain times in a certain building, worship of God breaks into your day at home, too.

So does prayer. Individually and as a couple, spending focused time with God should sometimes be spontaneous, sometimes planned. It should be relational and meaningful, not formulaic.

4. *A Christian home is based on God's purposes for you.* Maybe you dream of how your kids will grow up and what retirement will be like. But does your vision of the future match God's?

You're probably familiar with the concept of a mission statement. This clarification of purpose is as valuable for families as it is for corporations. Developing one is a wonderful place to start crafting your Christian home. These core values and guiding principles should be flexible but consistent. They can reflect not just what you want for yourselves and your children, but also outline how you want to influence the home in which your grand-children will be raised.

Christ-centered couples are driven by the hope of seeing Jesus one day. They avoid cluttering their eternal focus—and their homes—with possessions and people-pleasing.

When your marriage joins with God's purposes, you get a vibrant partnership. Instead of a contrived, rule-bound facade, you discover a rich and satisfying home life.

—Rob Jackson
Licensed Professional Counselor[4]

Chapter 3

TRUTH AND CONSEQUENCES

Our culture trains us poorly to pay the price for a committed, healthy relationship. We're hammered with statements like these:

"You're an army of one!"

"Look out for numero uno!"

"Have it your way!"

Small wonder marriages waver and stumble under the weight of such ranting about self-centered superiority.

Jim and Jolene, for example, weren't the least bit excited about counseling together. But here they finally were, in the therapist's office.

Both spouses were certain of their own rightness and the other's wrongness. They were a bit surprised when, without preliminaries, their counselor asked, "What would you rather do than fight?"

Before they could answer, the counselor instructed them to log the number of times they fought each day and to call him daily with the "score." He'd see them again in one week.

A week later, the counselor gave them another assignment: Log what fights are about. Jim and Jolene soon found that their arguments were too trivial to warrant continuing.

Six months later, they renewed their vows.

Wish you could do the same? Start by refusing to allow self-serving attitudes to snuff out the flame that once lit the rooms of your heart.

—Sam Kennedy
Licensed Marriage and Family Therapist[5]

Identifying Your Needs

Here are some questions to help you discover where you stand on this chapter's topic.

1. Which of the following is closest to your reaction when you hear that marriage is supposed to last a lifetime?
   ___ "Not anymore."
   ___ "That's absolutely right."
   ___ "Then I've already blown it."
   ___ "Impossible."
   ___ "Unfortunately, yes."
   ___ other _____

2. Which of the following do you think you understand as well as you need to? Which are you uncertain about?
   ___ God's view of divorce
   ___ why the Bible prohibits adultery
   ___ why God invented marriage
   ___ the biblical view of same-sex "marriage"
   ___ your spouse's opinions on these subjects

3. Which of the following do you think are good reasons to stay married? How would you rank them in order from least important to most? Why?
   ___ for the sake of the children
   ___ to avoid the embarrassment of divorce
   ___ because God said so
   ___ because your parents stayed married

___ due to peer or family pressure

___ for financial stability

4. Have you ever done something you knew was wrong? If so, why did you do it anyway? _____

_____

5. When it comes to marriage, what kinds of things do some spouses do that they probably know are wrong? Why? _____

_____

6. How much would someone have to pay you to take an "unbiblical" approach to marriage? Why?

___ $1,000,000,000

___ $1,000,000

___ $100,000

___ $10,000

___ no amount of money would be enough

___ no money would be necessary

___ other _____

Watching and Discussing the DVD

What happens when our take on marriage doesn't match God's perspective? Instead of asking how we can serve our spouses, we concentrate on getting our needs met. Sometimes those aren't needs at all—just wants.

Dr. Del Tackett returns in this DVD segment, challenging couples to live out the implications of God's view. How can we love and respect each

other more? How can we become one? How can we better reflect our
Creator's character?

The truth about marriage has consequences, and couples who live
accordingly will be glad they did.

After viewing the DVD, use questions like these to help you think
through what you saw and heard.

1. How would you describe the tone of Dr. Del Tackett's presentation on
   the DVD? Do you think it's appropriate for the subject? Why or why
   not?
   - exciting
   - sorrowful
   - awed
   - condemning
   - other _____

2. What happens when people defy God's laws or instructions in the
   following areas? How soon would you expect the consequences to be
   obvious?
   - gravity
   - adultery
   - being good stewards of creation
   - honoring parents
   - keeping a vow to stay married

3. Del is "the product of divorced parents." In your opinion, does that
   affect his credibility when talking about the results of ignoring God's
   view of marriage? If so, how?

4. How would you respond to someone who made the following statements? What kind of reply would you expect to get?

- "God has bigger things to worry about than how I treat my spouse."
- "I can't believe God would expect me to stay in an unhappy marriage."
- "My wedding vows don't count; I was too young when I made them."
- "Fantasies aren't real; they don't affect my marriage."

5. On a scale of 1 to 10 (10 highest), how would you rate the truthfulness of the following ideas? How would you rate their importance?
    - We don't need Satan to wreck our marriages; we're quite capable of doing it on our own.
    - There can be nothing more glorious on earth than following God's design.
    - There's no place for violence, verbal abuse, or rudeness in marriage.

6. According to Malachi 2:16, God hates divorce. How might each of the following people react to hearing this? How might they react to Del's explanation that this isn't just a pragmatic statement about the pain divorce brings, but grief over tearing apart the intimacy that reflects God's nature?
    - a divorce lawyer
    - a recently divorced person
    - a child whose parents divorced 20 years ago
    - a person considering divorce

7. After watching the DVD, which of these people do you feel most like? Why?
    - Del, when he confronted the couple having the adulterous affair

- the young woman who didn't think she could trust a man after her father left her mother
- the unfaithful spouses who seemed unaffected by God's Word

8. Del observes that God wants us to experience in marriage something of the wonder and beauty found in the relationship among the Persons of the Trinity—which leads to life, peace, and happiness. Which of the following steps would you take first to start experiencing that?
   - learning more about God's nature by reading the Bible
   - talking with your spouse about your relationship
   - asking God to help you understand what He wants your marriage to be
   - other _____

Bible Study

The wrath of God is being revealed from heaven against all the godlessness and wickedness of men who suppress the truth by their wickedness, since what may be known about God is plain to them, because God has made it plain to them. For since the creation of the world God's invisible qualities— his eternal power and divine nature—have been clearly seen, being understood from what has been made, so that men are without excuse. . . .

Therefore God gave them over in the sinful desires of their hearts to sexual impurity for the degrading of their bodies with one another. They exchanged the truth of God for a lie, and worshiped and served created things rather than the Creator—who is forever praised. Amen. (Romans 1:18-20, 24-25)

1. What is the "truth of God" when it comes to marriage?

2. What "lie" have some spouses exchanged it for?

3. Do you think the apostle Paul would be shocked by some current attitudes toward marriage, or would they remind him of his own culture? Why?

> *Why be captivated, my son, by an adulteress? Why embrace the bosom of another man's wife?*
>
> *For a man's ways are in full view of the LORD, and he examines all his paths.*
>
> *The evil deeds of a wicked man ensnare him; the cords of his sin hold him fast.*
>
> *He will die for lack of discipline, led astray by his own great folly.* (Proverbs 5:20-23)

4. What answers might an unfaithful spouse give to the questions in this passage? What answers are implied in many TV shows, movies, and popular songs?

5. If everything we do is "in full view of the LORD," why do so many people—even some Christians—seem to think He won't see what they do? If God's presence were observable, do you think there would be fewer extramarital affairs? Why or why not?

6. Based on what you see around you, when does sexual sin usually take its toll? Why might some believe they can get away with "evil deeds"?

Applying the Principles

Del Tackett warns of self-serving attitudes that can torpedo a marriage. So here's an exercise that helps you practice servanthood.

The object is to let your spouse tell you which favor in each of the following pairs would mean more to him or her, both as giver and receiver—and why. Then you can do the same. Don't debate; just share your opinions and listen.

CLEANING THE RING OUT OF THE BATHTUB

TAKING THE CAR TO GET THE OIL CHANGED

KEEPING THE BATHROOM SINK UNPLUGGED FOR SIX MONTHS

WRAPPING AND SHIPPING ALL THE PRESENTS NEXT CHRISTMAS

LISTENING CAREFULLY FOR 30 MINUTES

MAKING A WEEK'S WORTH OF SACK LUNCHES

BAKING TWO DOZEN COOKIES

BUYING TWO DOZEN COOKIES

TAKING A PET TO THE VETERINARIAN

RENTING A MACHINE AND CLEANING THE CARPET FOR THREE HOURS

GOING TO A "CHICK FLICK"

GOING TO THE HARDWARE STORE

BRINGING BOOKS BACK TO THE LIBRARY

MOWING THE LAWN

WASHING SPOUSE'S LAUNDRY

WASHING SPOUSE'S FEET

BALANCING THE
CHECKBOOK

TAKING PHOTOS OF
YOUR VALUABLE
POSSESSIONS FOR
INSURANCE PURPOSES

RECORDING
MISSED TV SHOWS
FOR A MONTH

TAKING OUT THE
GARBAGE FOR A
MONTH

When you've picked your favorite favors, each of you chooses two favors to do for the other, preferably this week.

Encouragement from a Counselor

What if self-serving attitudes have seriously damaged your relationship? Is it ever too late for a marriage?

Not if God has His way. Not if He's allowed to be an active part of creating healing and peace in the midst of your marital battles and woundedness. Even if there's only a shred of agreement left between you, it can be done.

The tiniest, flickering ray of hope can give off enough light to encourage your first, hesitant step toward loving and respecting each other. True, there can be some last-gasp attempts to vindicate angry motives and behaviors. But faith in God's eagerness to heal can furnish the energy you need to thrust your way past such roadblocks.

Perhaps the most insightful and poignant cry for restoration ever penned came from the heart of David, the Israelite king. It's in Psalm 51, which contains core phrases like these:

- "Have mercy" (vs. 1);
- "For I know my transgressions" (vs. 3);
- "You desire truth" (vs. 6);
- "Let me hear joy and gladness" (vs. 8);
- "Create in me a pure heart" (vs. 10);
- "Grant me a willing spirit" (vs. 12);
- "A broken and contrite heart, O God, you will not despise" (vs. 17).

That kind of attitude goes a long way toward rebuilding a marriage. David's confession also reminds us of three things:

- God's hand is extended to us.
- He wants us to heal.
- He will honor our cooperation and forgive our delinquencies.

Restoring your marriage may depend upon your willingness to forgive and honor one another. Still, if earnest self-examination and your attempts to make amends fall short, it will be sensible to concede that you could use help.

If your marriage is stressed to the point of collapse, dedicated professionals can save you time and frustration as you try to make a giant leap back into each other's trust and favor. The guidance of an experienced marriage "mender"—a Christian counselor—can shorten your journey appreciably.

Make no mistake: It won't be easy. Reconciliation poses a genuine challenge and demands your God-given best to produce results. Far too often when a marriage teeters on the edge of disaster, a late burst of stubbornness and pride takes hold; jaws lock in denying the need for anyone else's services.

But imagine the rewards of mending your relationship. They can be a powerful push, re-directing your thoughts and efforts toward regaining the satisfactions of your lost marital harmony. Just as love's flame flickers from careless inattention, it can be nurtured back to brightness by the decision to take action.

But what if you're the only partner willing to seek counseling? Should you go anyway?

Yes, yes, yes!

Many marriages have been rescued because one spouse took the initiative toward positive change. Often the partner who stayed home became curious and joined the counseling sessions, leading to a change of heart.

Thousands of couples have discovered the effectiveness of good counseling in rebuilding a marriage—even if they started as skeptics.

It's yours to experience—if you're willing to work at it.

—Sam Kennedy
Licensed Marriage and Family Therapist[6]

Chapter 4

ACHIEVING SPIRITUAL INTIMACY

Beth was overjoyed when her boyfriend, Don, became a Christian. She'd told him she couldn't marry a non-Christian. But she didn't know what lay ahead.

From the time he received Christ as his Savior, Don knew he was different. Within a few weeks he was talking to Beth—and anybody else who would listen—about Jesus and his new life.

Don was so enthusiastic, in fact, that Beth wasn't sure what to do with him. He wanted to pray with her—out loud! That was something she'd never done with a man. He thought they ought to bow in prayer at meals, even in restaurants.

When Don finally convinced Beth to marry him, she was still concerned about his exuberance over his new faith. She didn't feel comfortable with his desire to read the Bible together, much less pray.

Don didn't get it. Why wasn't Beth as thrilled as he was that they were both Christians? After all, the guys in his men's Bible study group all had been applauding his spiritual growth.

When he asked her about it, she tried to explain that her personal devotional life always had been just that—personal. Did they have to pray aloud together all the time?

Would praying together really make a difference in *your* marriage? What if one or both of you aren't comfortable with the idea?

—Lon Adams
Licensed Marriage and Family Therapist[7]

Identifying Your Needs

Here are some questions to ask yourself.

1. What's your response when you hear that spouses should pray together?
   ____ "That's for super-spiritual people."
   ____ "We tried that, but it didn't work for us."
   ____ "It would feel forced and fake."
   ____ "I know we should, but we never get around to it."
   ____ "We do, and I'm glad."
   ____ other _____

2. If you and your spouse got involved in a service project, what would you want it to be? Why?
   ____ serving food in a soup kitchen
   ____ visiting people in a nursing home
   ____ protesting an injustice
   ____ going on a mission trip to another country
   ____ short and sweet
   ____ other _____

3. Have you ever known a husband and wife who made ministry a priority in their marriage? If so, what were they like?
   ____ boring
   ____ admirable but out of our league
   ____ surprisingly normal
   ____ fun
   ____ obnoxious and hypocritical
   ____ other _____

4. What do you think is your spouse's most urgent prayer request right now? If you can't answer this question, how do you feel about that? _____

_____

5. On a scale of 1 to 10, how well do you and your spouse work as a team? How do you know? _____

_____

6. Do you think couples need a "mission statement"? Why or why not? _____

_____

Watching and Discussing the DVD

Plenty of Christians would say that faith should bring couples closer. But does it? Not if the only "faith-based" thing you do is sitting next to each other in church.

In this DVD segment, a battery of experts tell how to apply the principle of marital oneness to the spiritual side of your relationship. Gary Thomas urges husbands to pray for their wives; Stormie Omartian explains the benefits of praying and praising as a couple; Dr. Gary and Barb Rosberg deliver tips on praying together.

Finally, Drs. Les and Leslie Parrott tell how opening their home and taking on service projects has brought them closer—and can do the same for you.

After viewing the DVD, use questions like these to help you think through what you saw and heard.

1. Which kind of intimacy do you think is most important to the long-term success of a marriage: emotional, physical, or spiritual? Why? If you could have only one of them, which would you choose? Why? In an average week, about how much time do you devote to building each?

2. According to Gary Thomas, praying for your spouse creates empathy—helping you see the day through his or her eyes. If you prayed for your spouse on a typical weekday at the following times, what specifically would you pray about? How would you want your spouse to pray for you at those times?
   • 8:00 A.M.
   • noon
   • 5:15 P.M.
   • 10:00 P.M.

3. Gary notes that many men seem afraid to pray with their wives. What might be scaring them? Do you think most wives feel the same way about praying with their husbands? Why or why not?

4. Stormie Omartian says that praying and worshiping as a couple are the most powerful things you can do together. If you're already doing those things, which of the following obstacles did you overcome to get started? If not, which would be worth overcoming to give it a try? Which obstacle would you tackle first? Why?
   • lack of time
   • feeling embarrassed to pray or worship outside of a church meeting
   • not wanting to reveal deep emotions or personal thoughts
   • thinking it's not worth the effort
   • assuming it's only for super-spiritual people
   • not knowing how
   • other _____

5. Stormie observes that when you pray and praise together, strife is lifted from you. Dr. Gary and Barb Rosberg put it another way: It's hard to be mad at your mate when you pray together. Which of the following might account for that?
   - When you pray together, it forces you to agree.
   - Prayer and worship remind you that God is watching and listening.
   - You'd feel guilty about fighting after you pray.
   - Prayer and praise remind you that God is in charge, leading you to be humble.
   - Prayer and praise help you focus on your real priorities and common ground.
   - other _____

6. The Rosbergs note that prayer doesn't change the nature of God—it changes us. How would you like prayer to change you during the next six months?
   - I'd like to feel closer to my spouse.
   - I'd like to feel closer to God.
   - I'd like to feel my spouse and I are going in the right direction together.
   - other _____

7. The Rosbergs warn against using prayer with your spouse as a chance to preach at him or her. Which of the following prayers would you put in that category? Why?
   - "Lord, help my husband to be the man You want him to be."
   - "Thank You that You have raised up counselors to whom we should go when we are depressed."
   - "May we remember that Your Word tells us that a wife is to submit to her husband."
   - "We know that You will make it clear whether we should vacation in Hawaii or serve You building houses in Guatemala."

8. Drs. Les and Leslie Parrott say that practicing hospitality or otherwise serving together unites spouses, stimulates conversation between them, builds intimacy, and helps them fulfill their purpose. Which of these benefits appeals to you most? How might your hospitality or service benefit the recipients?

9. Which of the following suggestions from this session are you willing to try this week?
   - Take turns praying a sentence at a time.
   - Invite other couples into your home.
   - Sponsor a needy child together.
   - Do a "Shared Service in Secret" project.
   - Become a marriage mentor to another couple.
   - Ask another couple to mentor you.

Bible Study

> Now a man named Ananias, together with his wife Sapphira, also sold a piece of property. With his wife's full knowledge he kept back part of the money for himself, but brought the rest and put it at the apostles' feet.
> Then Peter said, "Ananias, how is it that Satan has so filled your heart that you have lied to the Holy Spirit and have kept for yourself some of the money you received for the land? Didn't it belong to you before it was sold? And after it was sold, wasn't the money at your disposal? What made you think of doing such a thing? You have not lied to men but to God."
> When Ananias heard this, he fell down and died. And great fear seized all who heard what had happened. Then the young men came forward, wrapped up his body, and carried him out and buried him.
> About three hours later his wife came in, not knowing what had hap-

pened. Peter asked her, "Tell me, is this the price you and Ananias got for the land?"

"Yes," she said, "that is the price."

Peter said to her, "How could you agree to test the Spirit of the Lord? Look! The feet of the men who buried your husband are at the door, and they will carry you out also."

At that moment she fell down at his feet and died. Then the young men came in and, finding her dead, carried her out and buried her beside her husband. Great fear seized the whole church and all who heard about these events. (Acts 5:1-11)

1. In what way did Ananias and Sapphira "live out their purpose together"? Why wasn't that an admirable thing?

2. What role do you think these spouses allowed God to have in their marriage? Where do you think they went wrong?

3. How do some couples try to "outvote" God and take their own direction in the following areas? What might be the consequences?
   - making decisions about having children
   - giving to the church
   - choosing movies to watch
   - buying cars
   - inviting others into their home

When Joseph and Mary had done everything required by the Law of the Lord, they returned to Galilee to their own town of Nazareth. And the child grew and became strong; he was filled with wisdom, and the grace of God was upon him.

Every year his parents went to Jerusalem for the Feast of the Passover. When he was twelve years old, they went up to the Feast, according to the custom. After the Feast was over, while his parents were returning home, the boy Jesus stayed behind in Jerusalem, but they were unaware of it.

Thinking he was in their company, they traveled on for a day. Then they began looking for him among their relatives and friends. When they did not find him, they went back to Jerusalem to look for him. After three days they found him in the temple courts, sitting among the teachers, listening to them and asking them questions. Everyone who heard him was amazed at his understanding and his answers. When his parents saw him, they were astonished. His mother said to him, "Son, why have you treated us like this? Your father and I have been anxiously searching for you."

"Why were you searching for me?" he asked. "Didn't you know I had to be in my Father's house?" But they did not understand what he was saying to them.

Then he went down to Nazareth with them and was obedient to them. But his mother treasured all these things in her heart. And Jesus grew in wisdom and stature, and in favor with God and men. (Luke 2:39-52)

4. What purpose did Mary and Joseph live out together in the above passage? What did it cost them to do that?

5. What made Mary and Joseph different from Ananias and Sapphira?

6. Did Mary and Joseph completely understand God's view of their purpose? If not, how did they manage to live it out anyway?

7. What was the result of this couple's teamwork?

Applying the Principles

Joining forces on a service project can bring you and your spouse closer. Why not start planning a project like that right now?

Look at the following columns. To help you decide what kind of project to tackle, pick an object from Column A, a place from column B, and a purpose from Column C. Then name your project and fill in the blanks with the details.

Once you've written down the next step you need to take, decide when and how you'll take it. If you're comfortable doing so, pray with your spouse for the success of your project—both for the sake of your beneficiary and your relationship.

Column A	*Column B*	*Column C*
Paint	Neighbor's house	Encouragement
Batch of cookies	School	Evangelism
Car	Jail	Political action
Pizza	Hospital	Hunger relief
Laptop	Church	Medical attention
Guitar	Nursing home	Hospitality
Hammer	Rescue mission	Stress relief
Blanket	Street corner	Fundraising
Bible	Food pantry	Transportation
Other _____	Other _____	Other _____

Name of project: "Operation _____"

Who benefits _____

What we'll spend _____

Time it will take _____

Starting date (approximate) _____

Ending date (approximate) _____

Materials needed _____

Advice needed _____

Person or organization to contact _____

Next step _____

Encouragement from a Counselor

A busy airline pilot, Nick found it tough to keep up with regular church attendance and personal prayer and Bible reading. His wife, Margaret, on the other hand, was more devoted to those disciplines. She wanted to pray before meals and on other occasions. The fact that praying together was so important to her made Nick feel uneasy—even irritated.

In premarital counseling, the two of them met with a mentor couple. Nick admitted that when it came to prayer, Margaret had expectations that he might not be interested in fulfilling. "I feel awkward doing that with her," he said of prayer. "Is it really better than praying by yourself?"

Deep down, Nick felt praying as a couple was something people did in "the olden days." What was the value in doing it now?

If you and your spouse are struggling with the idea of praying together, here are some things to keep in mind.

1. *Start with yourself.* A joint prayer and devotional life for a married couple works best when it's a natural outgrowth of each partner's personal time with God. If you haven't been praying much yourself, you might practice on your own for a while.

2. *Don't rush it.* If you're the more interested spouse, be patient. Praying together, like any family tradition you establish, must emerge from what both partners agree to and feel at ease with.

Remember Beth and Don? It took time for Beth to get on the same "page" as Don when it came to prayer. But as he matured in his faith and they found some devotional materials at the bookstore, she began to relax. Eventually their joint prayer and Bible reading times came more naturally.

In the case of Nick and Margaret, it took patience on Margaret's part to gently nudge Nick to consider his role as a spiritual leader. When he saw how important it was to her, he determined to learn more about praying together and to become more at ease with it. They began with "saying table grace," then added other requests Margaret had shown concern for. She was overjoyed at Nick's efforts, which in turn encouraged him.

3. *Start small.* Many couples, never having seen their parents pray together, find it an uneasy, challenging experience. Bill and Sue met the challenge by starting with what they knew.

They began by praying before meals. One day, after Sue's girlfriend at work had a miscarriage, Sue prayed about that right after Bill asked the blessing. That seemed easy enough. In time they began to kneel beside their bed at night and ask God to deal with other concerns. "Actually," Bill eventually told a friend, "it really hasn't been that hard. We even read the Christmas story together from the Bible, before opening our gifts."

4. *Use the resources available.* Can a mentoring couple or role model help you get started? Don's Bible study friends helped him get oriented, and his pastor suggested materials he and Beth could use.

Devotional books, pamphlets, and magazines can help take the pressure off by structuring your prayer times. Check your local Christian bookstore for examples.

As for Beth, she came to realize that praying together had its benefits. When Don prayed, her heart resonated with his. She liked the idea that he might be inspired and helped by hearing her concerns and praises, too.

She also came to see that praying together wasn't a test in which she had to impress Don with her spirituality. *After all,* she reminded herself, *God is the audience.*

—Lon Adams
Licensed Marriage and Family Therapist[8]

Chapter 5

MARRIAGE MYTHS AND EXPECTATIONS

Movie star Mickey Rooney said, "Marriage is like batting in baseball; when the right one comes along, you don't want to let it go by." It sounds good, until you realize that Mickey was married eight times. He must have had a lot of "good pitches" to swing at!

Not to be outdone, Glynn de Moss Wolfe, the world record holder of 26 marriages at the time, made a similar comparison. "Marriage is like stamp collecting," he said. "You keep looking to find that rare one."

Both men held what might be called the "needle in a haystack" view of picking a mate. According to this perspective, there's only one spouse with whom you could be happy. That person needs to be found even if it means discarding a spouse who no longer looks right for you.

Significant emotional pain lies in the wake of such a view. You won't find a "wrong needle" clause in the Bible that gives you an "out" if you conclude that your spouse isn't right for you. Instead you'll find in Malachi 2:15, "Do not break faith with the wife of your youth."

Marriage is not primarily about finding the right spouse. It's about being the right person.

—Glenn Lutjens
Licensed Marriage and Family Therapist[9]

Identifying Your Needs

Take a couple of minutes to fill out the following survey.

1. When you were growing up, which of the following TV shows had the most influence on your mental picture of marriage? What kind of influence did they have?

    ___ *Married with Children*

    ___ *Mad About You*

    ___ *The Cosby Show*

    ___ *Everybody Loves Raymond*

    ___ *Family Guy*

    ___ *According to Jim*

    ___ *The Brady Bunch*

    ___ other _____

2. Which of the following assumptions did you grow up with? Why? How do they compare with your spouse's expectations?

    ___ The husband keeps the car running and the house repaired.

    ___ The wife does most of the cooking.

    ___ Housekeeping chores should be shared about equally.

    ___ The husband keeps track of the money.

    ___ The wife should earn less than the husband.

    ___ The wife should stay home when the children are young.

3. Which of the following questions did you and your spouse-to-be discuss before marriage? Which did you not discuss but wish you had?

    ___ "Do you want to have children?"

    ___ "What church do you want to go to?"

    ___ "Which *Star Trek* captain do you like best?"

___ "How much should we save, spend, and give?"

___ "Are you a convicted felon?"

___ "How often do you want to visit your parents?"

4. Based on your experience, what do you think are the three biggest myths about marriage? _____

_____

5. What surprised you most about married life? _____

_____

6. Do you think premarital counseling should be required by law? Why or why not? _____

_____

Watching and Discussing the DVD

When you got married, what did you expect?

In this DVD segment, host Dr. Greg Smalley, along with marriage and family therapist Mitch Temple, talks about the disappointment and conflict that can arise from misconceptions of wedded bliss. Mitch reveals some top myths that can wreck marriages.

And both of these experts explain how aligning our expectations and beliefs with reality can keep us together.

After viewing the DVD, use questions like these to help you think through what you saw and heard.

1. Which of the following expectations did you bring to your marriage, only to find they didn't match reality?

- We'll go out as often as we did before we got married.
- She (or he) will always look this way.
- Our marriage will be like my parents'.
- All we need is love.
- other _____

2. From which of the following did you get most of your assumptions about marriage? If you have children, where do you think they'll get theirs?
    - TV and movies
    - your parents' teaching
    - your parents' example
    - the Bible
    - other _____

3. Mitch Temple talks about the marriage myth that says, "As long as we're happy, that's the most important thing." Mitch notes that commitment is more important to successful marriages. What role do you think happiness plays in marriage? Where does it come from?

4. Another marriage myth: "I made a mistake; I didn't marry my soul mate." How do you think the idea that there's only one "right" person for everyone got started? Is it less romantic to believe that a soul mate is something you become, not someone you find? Is it less spiritual? Why or why not?

5. Still another marriage myth: "I can change my spouse." What do you think would be Mitch's advice to Spouse A in each of the following situations?
    - Spouse A has always hated Spouse B's loud nose-blowing.
    - Spouse A wishes Spouse B would learn to balance a checkbook.

- Spouse A fears riding in the car with Spouse B, who is a careless driver.
- Spouse A rarely sees Spouse B, who spends six hours a day playing online video games.

6. How could each of the following myths "poison" a marriage? What truth would be an antidote to each statement?
    - "It doesn't matter how we treat each other if we're married."
    - "A crisis means our marriage is over."

7. One more marriage myth: "My attitude has nothing to do with it." How would you describe this attitude in three words? How would you describe in three words the attitudes reflected in each of the other myths? Which myth do you most need to question or reject this week?

Note: For more information on these and other marriage myths, see *The Marriage Turnaround* by Mitch Temple (Moody Publishers, 2009).

Bible Study

> *Many a man claims to have unfailing love, but a faithful man who can find? (Proverbs 20:6)*

1. Why do so many spouses promise that their love will never fail, only to "fall out of love"? How do your beliefs about love affect your ability to remain faithful?

It is a trap for a man to dedicate something rashly and only later to consider his vows. (Proverbs 20:25)

2. What percentage of couples do you think enter marriage "rashly" and later regret it? How could changing their expectations help to solve this problem?

Do not boast about tomorrow, for you do not know what a day may bring forth. (Proverbs 27:1)

3. What does this proverb have to say to a husband or wife who thinks, *I can change my spouse?*

He who works his land will have abundant food, but the one who chases fantasies will have his fill of poverty. (Proverbs 28:19)

4. Is a spouse with unrealistic expectations "chasing fantasies"? Why or why not?

Charm is deceptive, and beauty is fleeting; but a woman who fears the LORD is to be praised. (Proverbs 31:30)

5. If all husbands understood this verse when they got married, how might the infidelity rate be affected? How does it apply to wives as well?

When times are good, be happy; but when times are bad, consider: God has made the one as well as the other. Therefore, a man cannot discover anything about his future. (Ecclesiastes 7:14)

6. When you got married, did you think there were more good times ahead than bad ones? Did things turn out as you expected? How could this verse help a couple who's having a difficult year?

May your fountain be blessed, and may you rejoice in the wife of your youth. (Proverbs 5:18)

7. When was the last time you "rejoiced in the [spouse] of your youth" by recalling what attracted you when you first met? What are three of his or her qualities that led you to get married?

Applying the Principles

Do you expect the worst from your spouse? The best? How do your expectations affect your relationship?

Here's a way to find out. Complete the following sentences, each of which makes a prediction about your spouse's behavior during the coming year. Your spouse should do the same, predicting your behavior.

1. When a new, bigger, higher-resolution TV comes out, my spouse will . . .

2. Friends who are moving to an apartment will ask whether we want to adopt their cat, and my spouse will . . .

3. I will suggest a trip to see my relatives, and my spouse will . . .

4. The stock market will plunge, and my spouse will . . .

5. Our e-mail will stop working, and my spouse will . . .

6. Our church will take an offering for earthquake victims in China, and my spouse will . . .

7. I will discover a suspicious mole on my arm, leading my spouse to . . .

8. The price of gasoline will double, causing my spouse to . . .

9. The neighbors will get a dog that barks all the time, and my spouse will . . .

10. My spouse will inherit $10,000, leading him or her to . . .

When you're done, discuss the expectations that led you to make your predictions. Which ones are healthy? Which ones might not be completely justified? Which ones could be self-fulfilling prophecies? Which ones might you be better off without?

Encouragement from a Counselor

When you're single, you experience a range of contentment from low to high. When you marry, that range has the potential to become even wider in both directions. Greater contentment—or discontentment—can take place than in your single years.

If you and your loved one were unhappy as singles and expected marriage to fulfill your lives, you probably were greatly disappointed as your level of contentment dropped even lower. But if you sensed meaning and purpose in your lives individually and wanted to share them in a lifetime commitment, you likely experienced an increase in contentment. You might call this the Mine Theory of Mate Selection. You either find the "land mine" or the "gold mine" in marriage.

If you entered marriage hoping to finally find happiness in your mate, you probably didn't find it. Like a carpenter who may first have to remove the floor boards in order to shore up the rafters underneath, you may first need to find contentment individually.

During courtship, people are often sure they've found the "gold mine." Both spouses-to-be tend to get excited about this wonderful, new relationship. The fireworks of romance help them act kinder, more self-lessly, and more empathetically than they might when the fire fades.

We tend to fill in the gaps regarding the person we love. We assume during courtship that since he's willing to sit and listen to our feelings about life, he'll show the same concern after marriage when we want to talk about our frustrations. When he doesn't, we assume we married the wrong person.

In reality, he probably was not as wonderful as you thought he was before you married. On the other hand, he's probably not as terrible as you might now be thinking.

When the two of you walked down the aisle, each of you became the right person for the other. Yes, you may look back and second-guess your reasons. But you entered an arena in which learning to truly love someone takes a lifetime.

Is your spouse perfect? Not a chance. Welcome to the human race.

That's what Larry and Linda learned.

Larry no longer felt the excitement he had when he and Linda were dating. She didn't speak to him as sweetly as in the old days. And if her spending habits continued, the two of them would end up in the poor-house. Larry concluded that he'd made a mistake by marrying Linda.

When they entered counseling, Larry assumed Linda was not the woman for him. But he came to understand that even though Linda wasn't perfect, learning to love her was helping him grow as a spouse and become more lovable.

Larry might not have married Linda, knowing what he now knows about her. Yet he recognizes that beyond human decisions, God somehow works His purposes into the equation.

Larry no longer views marriage with a "needle in a haystack" mentality. He considers Linda as the one he's promised to love both in sickness and in health.

—Glenn Lutjens
Licensed Marriage and Family Therapist[10]

Chapter 6

WALKING IN THEIR SHOES

Dear Hazel:

My wife is totally opposite from me. I like to relax on the weekend. She wants me to work on the house the whole time and hates my watching TV.

Her need to talk is driving me crazy. I get annoyed when she asks me questions about work. We're constantly at odds over the temperature in the house.

Also, our choices in restaurants and movies don't come close to matching. I like barbecue and action films that she thinks are stupid. She likes Thai food and chick flicks that make me nauseous.

Since we're so different, I'm beginning to wonder if we should have gotten married at all.

Concerned in Colorado

Dear Hazel:

My husband is totally opposite from me. I wait for the weekend with the hope that he'll help me do some of the things I've been unable to do alone. I look forward to spending quality time as a family, but all he wants to do is sit in front of the TV and vegetate.

He doesn't share much about his work and seems annoyed when I ask him questions. I shiver when he's home because he always feels too hot and wants to keep the thermostat low. We can't even agree on the same TV shows, movies, or restaurants. I like Thai food and romantic comedies that he thinks are stupid. He likes martial arts movies and charred turkey legs that make me nauseous.

Since we're so different, I'm beginning to wonder if we should have gotten married at all.

Despondent in Denver

How can these spouses understand each other? It all begins with empathy.

—Romie Hurley
Licensed Professional Counselor[11]

Identifying Your Needs

Here are some questions to help define where you are on the topic of this session.

1. Which of the following do you think are good examples of empathy? Why?

_____ a near-stranger at church saying, "I know how you feel"

_____ your mother baking you cookies when you're not invited to a party

_____ President Bill Clinton saying, "I feel your pain"

_____ your spouse giving you a back rub when you've had a hard day

_____ Psalm 103:13-14

____ your dog staring dolefully at you when you're sad

____ other _____

2. On a scale of 1 to 10 (10 highest), how well do you think your spouse understands you in each of the following areas? How do you know?

____ your fears

____ your dreams

____ your feelings about God

____ your feelings about work

____ your favorite dessert

3. On a scale of 1 to 10 (10 highest), how well do you think you understand your spouse in each of the following areas? How do you know?

____ his or her fears

____ his or her dreams

____ his or her feelings about God

____ his or her feelings about work

____ his or her favorite dessert

4. What's one thing you've done in the last month to help you better understand your spouse? _____

5. If you haven't done anything, why is that? If you have, did it work? Why or why not? _____

_____

Watching and Discussing the DVD

What's it like to be your spouse? If that's beyond your powers of imagination, you'll find it hard to understand him or her.

Empathy—the ability to "feel for" and identify with someone else—goes a long way toward improving practically everything in a marriage, from communication to sex to spiritual closeness.

In this DVD segment, Gary Thomas notes that God's empathy for us is a model of how spouses should treat each other. Drs. Les and Leslie Parrott explain how our mates need more than our sympathy, how empathy creates safety, and how we can gain understanding by mentally "trading places" with our spouses.

After viewing the DVD, use questions like these to help you think through what you saw and heard.

1. How do you feel when you hear the following? Why?
   - "I know how you feel."
   - "You shouldn't feel that way."
   - "Tell me how you feel."
   - "My heart goes out to you."
   - "I can't imagine how you must feel."

2. Gary Thomas points out that God understands us as no one else does. What difference does it make to you that God knows the following?
   - the number of hairs on your head
   - your thoughts
   - how long you'll live
   - the sins you've committed
   - your prayers
   - what you go through every day

3. Which of the following do you think is most like God's empathy for you? Why? Which is most like the empathy one spouse needs to have for another?
   - the compassion a pet owner has for a dog or cat
   - the pity a passerby has for a homeless person

- the protectiveness a parent has for a child
- the understanding old friends have of each other
- other _____

4. Read Matthew 23:37 and Luke 23:32-35. How did Jesus show his empathy for people in these passages? Based on His example, how would you show understanding for your spouse in the following situations?
    - He or she learns of a close friend's sudden death.
    - He or she seems to be losing faith in God.
    - He or she lashes out verbally at you.

5. Drs. Les and Leslie Parrott say they'd like to give you a box containing the power of empathy. If there really were such a thing, how much do you think a one-month supply would cost? What would the packaging claim? What ingredients might be listed? What warnings about side effects might it include?

6. According to the Parrotts, how is empathy different from sympathy? Which one is "all heart," and which involves heart, mind, and action? How might the responses of a sympathetic spouse and an empathetic one differ in each of the following situations?
    - A husband dreads spending Thanksgiving with his in-laws, who've never approved of his "low-class" upbringing. How does the wife respond?
    - A wife has to go on a low-sugar diet due to diabetes. How does the husband respond?
    - A husband announces that he wants to become a policeman, even though his wife thinks it would be stressful and dangerous. How does the wife respond?
    - A wife is being overworked and underpaid by a clueless boss. How does the husband respond?

7. The Parrotts explain that empathy creates a safe, comfortable place for both spouses. What's one way in which your mate seems to understand you better than anyone else does? When does that mean the most to you?

8. The Parrotts also advise that you need to understand yourself before you can understand your spouse. Which of the following best describes your reaction to that?
    • "I don't want to get in touch with my feelings."
    • "I'd rather do both at the same time."
    • "It makes sense, but I can't do it alone."
    • "My spouse has helped me understand myself."
    • other _____

Bible Study

> *Rejoice with those who rejoice; mourn with those who mourn.*
> *(Romans 12:15)*

1. How would you follow this verse's principle in each of the following situations?
    • Your spouse just got home from a job you know he or she hates.
    • Your spouse just won an award you've never been able to win.
    • You and your spouse are on the same diet; he or she gained three pounds this week, and you lost four.

> *Like one who takes away a garment on a cold day, or like vinegar poured on soda, is one who sings songs to a heavy heart. (Proverbs 25:20)*

2. How does this verse provide a picture of empathy—or lack of it? If you're perky and optimistic and your spouse tends toward gloom and pessimism, how can you apply the wisdom of this proverb?

> *If a man loudly blesses his neighbor early in the morning, it will be taken as a curse. (Proverbs 27:14)*

3. If one spouse is a "morning person" and the other is a "night owl," how can each show sensitivity to the other's needs? What if one is an extrovert and the other an introvert? What if one is a careful planner and the other likes to be spontaneous?

> *When Mary reached the place where Jesus was and saw him, she fell at his feet and said, "Lord, if you had been here, my brother would not have died."*
>
> *When Jesus saw her weeping, and the Jews who had come along with her also weeping, he was deeply moved in spirit and troubled. "Where have you laid him?" he asked.*
>
> *"Come and see, Lord," they replied.*
>
> *Jesus wept.*
>
> *Then the Jews said, "See how he loved him!" (John 11:32-36)*

4. Why did Jesus cry? Was it because He thought Lazarus was gone forever or because He empathized with the grief of Mary and her friends?

5. From what you know of Jesus, would you say He really understands what it means to be human? If so, how did He get that understanding?

6. How does the experience of Jesus provide a model for someone who wants to better understand his or her spouse?

Applying the Principles

The Parrotts suggest mentally trading places with your spouse to better empathize with him or her.

To help you start thinking like your spouse, here's a word-matching exercise. For each word in the first column, what second-column word would your spouse most likely associate with it? To show your answer, draw a line from each word in the first column to one in the second column. Your spouse should do the same on your behalf. You can use the words in the second column as many times as you like.

Word 1	Word 2
Gun	Danger
Chocolate	Safety
Bible	Disgust
Snake	Fun
Anniversary	Boredom
Intimacy	Comfort
Doctor	Joy
Missionary	Harsh
Father	Gentle
Vacation	Stress
Career	Winning
Wedding	Losing
Dollar	Happiness
Hair	Disappointment

When you're done, discuss the results. What fears, likes, and dislikes have you uncovered? Were there any surprises?

How could better understanding and caring about your spouse's feelings—concerning guns or hair, for example—make a difference in your relationship?

What words could you add to the first column that would reflect something you'd like to know about your spouse? If possible, add those words and do the exercise again.

Here's another way to gain empathy with your spouse. Try writing your mate a letter in which you imagine what tomorrow will be like for him or her, including the three potentially most stressful times and how your spouse might feel about them. Then, if you like, pray together about those times and feelings.

Encouragement from a Counselor

Here's how that advice columnist might reply to the two letters at the beginning of this session.

Dear Concerned and Despondent,

Start by remembering what drew you to one another in the first place. Did you once *like* the fact that your spouse was more outgoing than you were, or got you to try new foods or films, or was willing to complain about being overcharged when you weren't?

Did you really not notice the differences before you got married? Or did other qualities seem more important? If the latter was the case, are some of those qualities still there?

If you haven't already, take some personality tests such as the Myers-Briggs Type Indicator and the Taylor-Johnson Temperament Analysis. These are available from counselors. After taking the tests, discuss your individual qualities and how each of you brings balance and perspective to the relationship. This can actually be fun instead of dividing you.

It's time to have a heart-to-heart talk, preferably when both of you are relaxed and undisturbed by children, work, or phone. Pick a place that's conducive to talking. Consider this a brainstorming session, a time to let your spouse know that you intend to find ways for the two of you to get closer—and still be your unique selves.

Decide to help each other get what you want and need in life, and state that intention. Remember that the quality of a relationship is a function of how well it meets the needs of both parties.

Prepare for this meeting by thinking through what you want to say, so that you will share only what's true and comes from the heart. Plan to tell your spouse about the things you admire and appreciate in him or her. Discuss in a positive way the things you miss doing together. Ask what you can do to help get some of those things back.

Apologize for the ways in which you haven't been there for each other. Ask what you can do to help one another relax.

Show an interest in really knowing one another. Intimacy has been defined as "into me see." It's important to "see into" each other in order to understand. And understanding is what empathy is all about.

—Romie Hurley
Licensed Professional Counselor[12]

NOTES

1. Adapted from Betty Jordan, "How Can Faith Keep Us Together?" in *Complete Guide to the First Five Years of Marriage* (Carol Stream, Ill.: Focus on the Family/Tyndale House Publishers, 2006), p. 279.

2. Ibid, pp. 279-281.

3. Adapted from Rob Jackson, "What Does a Christ-centered Home Look Like?" in *Complete Guide to the First Five Years of Marriage*, p. 288.

4. Ibid, pp. 288-291.

5. Adapted from Sam Kennedy, "Is It Ever Too Late for a Marriage?" in *Complete Guide to the First Five Years of Marriage*, pp. 412-413.

6. Ibid, pp. 411-413.

7. Adapted from Lon Adams, "Do We Have to Pray Together?" in *Complete Guide to the First Five Years of Marriage*, p. 285.

8. Ibid, pp. 285-287.

9. Adapted from Glenn Lutjens, "Did I Marry the Wrong Person?" in *Complete Guide to the First Five Years of Marriage*, p. 60.

10. Ibid, pp. 60-62.

11. Adapted from Romie Hurley, "How Can I Understand My Spouse's Personality?" in *Complete Guide to the First Five Years of Marriage*, pp. 27-28.

12. Ibid, pp. 28-30.

About Our DVD Presenters

Essentials of Marriage: Higher Love

Stormie Omartian is a best-selling Christian author with more than eight million copies of her books *The Power of a Praying Wife, The Power of a Praying Parent, The Power of a Praying Husband, The Power of a Praying Woman,* and *The Power of Praying Together* in print. *The Power of a Praying Husband* received the Gold Medallion award in 2002. Currently living in Nashville, Stormie and her husband, Michael, have been married for over 25 years and have three children.

Dr. Les Parrott III is a professor of psychology and codirector with his wife, **Dr. Leslie Parrott**, of the Center for Relationship Development at Seattle Pacific University. He is a fellow in medical psychology at the University of Washington School of Medicine and an ordained minister in the Church of the Nazarene. Les earned his M.A. in theology and his Ph.D. in clinical psychology from Fuller Theological Seminary. Les has written more than 10 books, including *Questions Couples Ask, Becoming Soul Mates,* and *Saving Your Marriage Before It Starts* (all cowritten with Leslie).

Dr. Gary and Barb Rosberg, cofounders of America's Family Coaches, host a nationally syndicated daily radio program and have conducted conferences on marriage and family relationships in more than 100 cities across the country. The Rosbergs have written more than a dozen prominent marriage and family resources, including *The 5 Love Needs of Men & Women* (a Gold Medallion finalist) and *Divorce-Proof Your Marriage* (a Gold Medallion winner). Gary earned his Ed.D. from Drake University and has been a marriage and family counselor for more than 25 years. Married more than 30 years, the Rosbergs live outside Des Moines, Iowa, and have two married daughters and four grandchildren.

Dr. Greg Smalley earned his doctorate in clinical psychology from Rosemead School of Psychology at Biola University. He also holds master's degrees in counseling psychology (Denver Seminary) and clinical psychology (Rosemead School of Psychology). Greg is president of Smalley Marriage Institute, a marriage and family ministry in Branson, Missouri, and serves as chairman of the board of the National Marriage Association. Greg has published more than 100 articles on parenting and relationship issues. He is the coauthor of *The DNA of Parent-Teen Relationships* (with his father, Gary Smalley) and *The Men's Relational Toolbox* (with his father and his brother, Michael). Greg, his wife, Erin, and their three children live in Branson, Missouri.

Gary Thomas is a writer and the founder/director of the Center for Evangelical Spirituality, a speaking and writing ministry that combines Scripture, history, and the Christian classics. His books include *Sacred Marriage, Authentic Faith* (winner of the Gold Medallion award in 2003), and *Seeking the Face of God.* Gary has spoken in 49 states and four countries and has served as the campus pastor at Western Seminary, where he is an adjunct professor. Gary, his wife, Lisa, and their three kids live in Bellingham, Washington.

Mitch Temple is a licensed marriage and family therapist and author of *The Marriage Turnaround.* He holds two graduate degrees, in ministry and in marriage and family therapy, from Southern Christian University. Mitch currently serves as the director of the marriage department at Focus on the Family in Colorado Springs. He has conducted intensives nationwide for couples on the brink of divorce and has served as a family, pulpit, and counseling minister in churches for a total of 23 years. He was director of pastoral care, small groups, family ministry, and a counseling center at a large church for 13 years. He and his wife, Rhonda, have been married for more than 24 years and have three children.

Dr. Del Tackett is president of Focus on the Family Institute and senior vice president of Focus on the Family. He is also the architect and chief spokesperson for Focus on the Family's *The Truth Project,* a nationwide initiative designed to bring the Christian worldview to the body of Christ. He and his wife live in Colorado Springs, Colorado.

FOCUS ON THE FAMILY®

Welcome to the Family

Whether you purchased this book, borrowed it, or received it as a gift, we're glad you're reading it. It's just one of the many helpful, encouraging, and biblically based resources produced by Focus on the Family® for people in all stages of life.

Focus began in 1977 with the vision of one man, Dr. James Dobson, a licensed psychologist and author of numerous best-selling books on marriage, parenting, and family. Alarmed by the societal, political, and economic pressures that were threatening the existence of the American family, Dr. Dobson founded Focus on the Family with one employee and a once-a-week radio broadcast aired on 36 stations.

Now an international organization reaching millions of people daily, Focus on the Family is dedicated to preserving values and strengthening and encouraging families through the life-changing message of Jesus Christ.

Focus on the Family MAGAZINES

These faith-building, character-developing publications address the interests, issues, concerns, and challenges faced by every member of your family from preschool through the senior years.

| FOCUS ON THE FAMILY® MAGAZINE | FOCUS ON THE FAMILY CLUBHOUSE JR.® Ages 4 to 8 | FOCUS ON THE FAMILY CLUBHOUSE® Ages 8 to 12 | FOCUS ON THE FAMILY CITIZEN® U.S. news issues |

For More INFORMATION

ONLINE:
Log on to
FocusOnTheFamily.com
In Canada, log on to
FocusOnTheFamily.ca

PHONE:
Call toll-free:
800-A-FAMILY
(232-6459)
In Canada, call toll-free:
800-661-9800

Rev. 12/08

More Great Resources
from Focus on the Family®

Complete Guide to the First Five Years of Marriage: Launching a Lifelong, Successful Relationship

Thousands of couples have asked the counselors at Focus on the Family for insight into money, communication, and a host of other issues. Now their collective wisdom is available for you in this handy reference book, the *Complete Guide to the First Five Years of Marriage*. Hardcover.

Blueprints for a Solid Marriage
by Dr. Steve Stephens

Marriage, like a house, requires time, effort, and regular maintenance. Whether you are building the foundation, making repairs or needing to remodel your relationship, *Blueprints for a Solid Marriage* helps any time-strapped couple assess their relationship and then take action with an easy-to-follow plan and fun "marriage improvement projects." Hardcover.

Your Marriage Masterpiece: Discovering God's Amazing Design for Your Life Together
by Al Janssen

Your Marriage Masterpiece takes a fresh look at the exquisite design God has for your marriage and brings to light the reasons your union was intended to last a lifetime. You will examine passion, adventure, commitment, and other principles that will make your marriage a masterpiece. And you will be reminded of God's love and passion for you and your spouse. Paperback.